Early Days and Pioneering

The British Electric Traction Company was a powerhouse, literally. It was set up to build tramway systems, usually including electric power stations to power them. But tramways are expensive to build and in the twentieth century BET set up a subsidiary – named the British Automobile Traction company, or BAT – to establish new bases, using the new-fangled motor buses.

One of its ventures was based in Macclesfield, established in 1913. It did well and expanded north to Stockport, west to Northwich and east to the High Peak. Its green buses carried a 'BRITISH' name on the side and although the buses were primitive and the roads weren't much better, Macclesfield soon became a key operating base for the company.

Creating new services wasn't straightforward, there was no research data to use. Inspectors would drive along roads to see if they were fit to take a bus, decide if the area would make a bus route pay, and if they thought it did, licences would be applied for. In rural areas local authorities, who issued licences until the 1930 Road Traffic Act, encouraged anyone to use buses to open isolated areas. In the towns it was different, the local authority might have their own bus or tram operation and they didn't welcome competition from this new company. Many was the battle over the years between North Western and Stockport, or Manchester, or Warrington, or the SHMD Board.

The 'British' operation got to the point that it was decided that one single outfit managing buses scattered across England, managed from London, was unwieldy. So, on 23 April 1923 a new company was formed to take over the 'Macclesfield branch'. It was named the North Western Road Car Company Limited, and its head office was Charles Street in Stockport, which had already become a more significant centre for the business. The colour scheme for the buses was changed to red and cream.

The move paid off: within a short time, the shape of North Western territory assumed the one it kept for the next fifty years. Some of the growth was organic, opening up new routes like ice patterns crossing a frozen pond; others came from buying businesses such as Sharp's of Manchester, whose service from that city to Woodford was snapped up in 1936.

The biggest influences on where North Western buses ran were politics and negotiation. NWRCC wasn't the only bus company in the territory twixt Trent and Mersey, but North Western's hand became strong both by being part of a bigger national empire; and by the influence of the railways.

Two national groups were expanding rapidly; the British Automobile Traction group and rivals Tilling. To avoid wasteful competition, they decided to pool many of their interests in (stand by for the inspired name) the Tilling and British Automobile Traction company (TBAT). This meant that border disputes with other companies, such as Crosville to the west and Potteries to the south, were resolved over claret instead of in a traffic court.

By the 1930s, only ten years after its founding, North Western was the main provider of bus services across a patch of 600 square miles of the southern end of the North West. It was a remarkable rise.

NORTH WESTERN
BUSES

PAUL WILLIAMS

AMBERLEY

Acknowledgements

I must thank the Museum of Transport Greater Manchester for most of the photographs in this book, selected from its extensive archive. Royalties from this book are being donated to the Museum, which is not only an excellent facility telling the story of Greater Manchester's road passenger transport, but also houses a selection of restored North Western Road Car Company buses. It's open Wednesdays, weekends and Bank Holidays and you can find out more about it by going online to: www.motgm.uk.

Other photographs came from Alan Snatt, Richard Higgs, June Beeston, Warren Vipond, Philip Edwards and Andrew Harvey-Adams; and although space precluded reproducing all bar a couple of the reminiscences I received, I want to thank everyone who responded to my appeal for stories that were published in Cheshire and Derbyshire local newspapers at the start of the project.

This book is dedicated to Dawn, Heather and Adam who tolerate my bus eccentricities.

First published 2020

Amberley Publishing
The Hill, Stroud
Gloucestershire, GL5 4EP

www.amberley-books.com

Copyright © Paul Williams, 2020

The right of Paul Williams to be identified as the Author of this work has been asserted in accordance with the Copyrights, Designs and Patents Act 1988.

ISBN 978 1 4456 9954 7 (print)
ISBN 978 1 4456 9955 4 (ebook)

British Library Cataloguing in Publication Data.
A catalogue record for this book is available from the British Library.

Origination by Amberley Publishing.
Printed in the UK.

Contents

Introduction

From 1923 to the 1970s, the North Western Road Car Company Limited (NWRCC) was one of the most famous bus companies in the north of England. Its services served a swathe of territory from Northwich in the west to the fringes of Sheffield in the east, and from Rochdale in the north to Matlock in the south.

Its end came because many of the profitable services were in Greater Manchester; and SELNEC wanted to buy the part of North Western that was in its area. What was left wasn't viable, so North Western's owner, NBC, split the remainder up between neighbours Trent and Crosville. A few National Express coaches based in Manchester carried North Western names for a few years, then faded away. The name lay dormant until NBC was parcelled up ready for privatisation, and the southern area of Ribble based on Merseyside needed a new name. The North Western name was revived for a few years until the company was snapped up by an international conglomerate, and that was that.

Except it wasn't. North Western lives on in memories, in photos like the ones in this book, in a collection of preserved buses and coaches, and even – at a location I'd rather not disclose – at a bus stop, in its original location, in red and cream, which says 'BUS STOP BY REQUEST NWRCC'.

Bus companies tend to be pigeonholed. They're city fleets threading between terraces and factories; or they're country buses, earning a meagre living from infrequent services to villages; or they're prestigious, touring far and wide and thundering down motorways to London. But North Western was all of these. It had a coach fleet running expresses from Manchester to London by day or by night. It dominated interurban hourlies across Cheshire and South Manchester; and its buses were liable to pop up in the most unexpected places in places like Middleton Top, or Lower Peover. The urban services subsidised the country buses, and the expresses and tours – as well as being profitable – gave the name 'North Western' a cachet that was respected all over the country. But like the stones in an arch, if you took away one piece the rest didn't work. When SELNEC bought the services in Greater Manchester, the rural services weren't sustainable, and the expresses couldn't work without sharing the bus garages of their more humble mates. It was inevitable that North Western couldn't live on. And yet, while other former bus companies are un-mourned, letters from the author to some local newspapers elicited an outpouring of happy memories.

This book doesn't set out to be a history of North Western. It's simply a reminiscence, remembering the company with rose-tinted spectacles and a sturdy anorak – it gets cold up above Buxton.

War and its Aftermath

North Western entered the war as an important provider of public transport. Most of the operating area was rural so unlikely to be troubled by enemy air action, but some was in the Manchester conurbation so might be targeted by the Luftwaffe.

More pressing issues hit North Western. From the start, the two preoccupations became fuel – or the lack of it – and the blackout. Fuel rationing was imposed, as was a set of government restrictions on bus mileage, which was set to no more than the company had run in 1938. But as NWRCC was growing that was an effective cut in itself. Then restrictions closed evening entertainment such as cinemas, temporarily; cutting out useful after-peak revenue. The blackout discouraged evening passengers and was a menace for the company. In cities, although streetlights were extinguished and homes weren't allowed to show a light, there were just enough dimmed headlamps on other vehicles and torches held by pedestrians that you could normally work out where the middle of the road was. But in rural areas there was no light, no traffic and no chance of spotting that dry stone wall next to the lane. Charles Street Works' workload increased, and so did the rate of platform staff sickness.

All vehicles were given white paint markings, and North Western's cream bus roofs were covered in grey to make them less visible from the air. That was about all the paint North Western's buses got until 1945, as Charles Street concentrated on just keeping the fleet going whilst skilled staff from all garages joined up with HM Forces 'for the duration'.

In 1939 North Western had entered the war with a modern fleet, well-maintained and with a smooth-running traffic operation. In 1945 the buses were tired with too few replacements entering the fleet during the war years. Rationing of fuel and materials persisted and staff wages had started to fall behind.

Post-War Boom and Clouds on the Horizon

Orders were placed to update the fleet. The key supplier in the 1940s was the same one as in the late 1930s – Bristol, originally an offshoot of the bus operating company of that name. Bristol was an operator that, in the early part of the century, had tried the frail buses of the time and decided that it knew what it wanted from its buses, so would build them. The result was unsophisticated but rugged and once it was coupled with the legendary Gardner diesel engine, a fleet engineer's dream. So NWRCC adopted Bristol buses, and their reliability was one of the reasons North Western managed to get through the war without a serious crisis.

Every bus company had the same post-war fleet replacement problems, so in a seller's market NWRCC also bought Leylands especially for its double deck fleet. This was a good job, for in 1948 it was announced that the Tilling group, of which Bristol was part, was to be nationalised. As part of the deal, Bristol buses would no longer be available to privately owned bus companies. The door to the Bristol factory closed.

But no matter, there was a post-war boom, with a pent-up demand for travel accompanied by continuing fuel rationing for private cars. So not only were North Western's buses full, but the coaching business – already an important feature of the company's business – really took off. Services from Lower Mosley Street bus station, in Manchester, were full to bursting every weekend and sometimes, in Wakes Weeks, in the week too.

The busiest long-distance service was the X60 between Manchester and Blackpool, jointly operated between North Western, Ribble and Lancashire United. During the summer at the weekend, the 50-mile service was booked for a fifteen-minute frequency. However, in practice on many Saturdays there'd be a constant stream of buses headed for the coast. Although all three operators were big companies, there would be shortages, and depot foremen from Northwich to Matlock would be urged to dig out anything from the back of the garage to shift the crowds.

There were other 'prestige' services such as the Tyne-Tees-Mersey linking Liverpool and Newcastle via Manchester, Leeds and Middlesbrough; buses usually worked all the way through, but crews tended to not get too far from their own patch. This meant that the driver could bring home someone else's coach; and given the varying vehicle purchase policies of the joint operators, some eccentric options could be presented to the North Western driver!

By the 1950s, North Western was part of the regional fabric. Its buses were at the heart of many a household's shopping or commuting plans, and its cream coaches were the transport of choice for holidays and high days. But trouble was brewing. Just as it seemed NWRCC was a permanent fixture, passenger numbers began to fall. At first it just seemed to be a blip, but it soon became a slope and then a steep drop.

There were several reasons, but only one outcome. Petrol rationing ended, whilst it became easier to buy a car as the government stopped forcing manufacturers to export to earn foreign income. TV arrived which killed local cinemas and the evening bus services that cinemagoers used, and rising staff costs, caused by full employment and rising fuel tax, made it harder to balance the books. Fares rose, which chased away more passengers, and the spiral of falling passenger numbers began.

And So To the End

By the late 1950s, NWRCC was starting to look frayed around the edges. Passenger numbers were in decline and fuel duty was going up. Full employment made it harder to recruit and keep staff on low wages and shift work. The company retained the loyalty of most of its staff and most of its passengers, but although the Greater Manchester services were still profitable a pruning exercise began on rural services that was to last until the end of the company's existence.

Economies were sought in other ways. Gradually the paint scheme was simplified, with cream roofs giving way to less-fading red; black lining-out was reduced and then disappeared; and, in a few cases, the entire bus was simply painted red with no cream at all, which was very ugly and thankfully not adopted.

Smaller engines were tried, single rear tyres (fun in the rain), and one-man operation. The company made a profit, helped by the Manchester services and the coach business, but the Chief Accountant's brow was getting more furrowed by the year. Maintenance standards started to slip and a few PSV71 forms, which put a bus off the road until the faults were rectified, were dished out by Ministry Inspectors, but in the 1960s North Western's position started to improve and led to a fairly brief 'Indian summer'.

In 1968, two milestones happened for North Western – one was positive, the other turned out to be very negative. The first was that the company's beloved Bristol buses were back on the market, thanks to lobbying by an MP from that city named Tony Benn. North Western ordered forty as soon as it was possible and followed up with orders for more until the end of the company's existence. The second development was darker: in Westminster, MPs passed something called the Transport Act 1968. It was to lead to the end of North Western.

North Western's owner – the British Electric Traction concern, or 'BET' – knew about the looming Transport Act and decided to get out of the bus business. North Western became part of the publicly owned National Bus Company (NBC), although on the surface nothing changed. But the following year a revolution was afoot on North Western's doorstep: under the Act, the municipalities of the area around Manchester were merged into a new Passenger Transport Executive, SELNEC, with powers to run bus services, subsidise rail operations and plan the region's transport strategy.

Almost all North Western's profitable bus services were in this area but now, instead of a bevy of municipalities to negotiate with over traffic sharing, it faced an orange behemoth. SELNEC wasn't content to stand still – it saw itself as more than just a bus operator. It wanted to change things, it wanted to experiment with electric buses, it wanted to build a new 'Picc-Vic' underground rail tunnel under Manchester City Centre; and it wanted to control all passenger transport in its area.

So SELNEC approached NBC and made an offer for all the North Western operations in its area. This was the most profitable part of NWRCC. So NBC took the money, then pondered what to do with the rural bus operations in Cheshire and Derbyshire, plus the express coach business. It transferred the west area, basically the Cheshire patch, to old rival Crosville; and the east area, basically Derbyshire, to BET neighbour Trent.

Over the course of a messy few weeks at the start of 1972, as the legal and licensing issues were dealt with, North Western was carved up. The coaching business remained but it didn't last, with the livery soon changed to National Express white and the head office moved to the Preston HQ of Ribble. By the end of the decade the magical 'North Western' name on coaches thundering along the M6 had been replaced by the more prosaic 'National Travel West'. Trent and Crosville embarked on a crash course to repaint all their inherited buses within a year, while SELNEC took its time and the last red buses disappeared around the end of 1976.

Depots, Garages, Kit and Tales

Unlike northern neighbour Ribble, North Western never built a huge bureaucracy and its Stockport head office – across the street from the garage – was modest. It preferred to give authority to its network of garage heads, given the uninspiring title 'Running Foreman'. This led to surprising levels of autonomy, although the story that when Trent took over the Derbyshire garages they found a car repair business occupying the tiny Castleton shed is apocryphal.

Charles Street Works was equipped for overhauls up to and including severe accident repairs. Other garages did routine maintenance but repaints were typically sent to Stockport. While the bus (sorry, car – North Western was a 'Road Car' company and so its vehicles were 'cars') spent time in the works, one of a pool of vehicles would be loaned. These would usually be more disreputable specimens, so garages were typically pleased to get their 'own' vehicle back.

Talking of retrieving vehicles, the summer holiday season would cause phone calls out from Stockport on Friday to find out what was mobile and could be loaned for express services, even double-deckers. And if a fellow-BET company coach was visiting Manchester on a long layover, NWRCC wasn't above 'borrowing' it for a quick trip to Blackpool or Leeds! On occasions coaches simply went missing, until enquiries (and evasive answers on the phone) teased out the admission that a Northwich coach was currently out running a Matlock track on the 4 to Derby…

If a car was unlucky enough to break down or have an accident, then Charles Street might send the 'Brab' or later the 'Mat'. The 'Brab' (probably short for 'Brabazon' after the impressive airliner of that name) was a Bristol L5G bus whose old body had been removed and a new breakdown truck body built at Charles Street. By the 1960s it was worn out, so an ex-military AEC 'Matador' lorry was purchased and again Charles Street built a recovery truck body, this time an elegant piece of work based on parts from the Alexander Y-type body.

For smaller jobs most depots had a Land Rover; a sensible choice given the company's territory. But as Chris Burnell relates, it wasn't a foolproof option:

> Around 1971 when I was a "fitter improver" at Urmston, the six o'clock start was to fix the defect logs from the night before. Easy stuff, handbrake adjustments, bulbs out, wipers not working… One morning a driver told me his bus wouldn't start – 941, a

Reliance. Anyway, I jumped in the Land Rover and drove round to 941, hooked up the towing chain and raised the rear door on the van so I could see the driver. I told him I'd pull him down the garage and when he fired, he should flash the lights and I'd stop.

Off we went, and as he dropped the clutch I felt the pull and I heard his engine fire up. I stopped the Land Rover, but what I didn't know was that 941 was on the defect log with a defective handbrake. My last sight through the raised tailgate was of 941 ploughing into the back of my Land Rover! This resulted in my rear tail hatch going through his windscreen with the driver using both hands on the handbrake and pushing the footbrake that didn't work without building up air pressure. 941 pushed me up the garage with bits of windscreen, front panel and Land Rover all over the garage floor. Chargehand Tommy Middleton came in at 7.30 am and I told him what had happened. He kept a straight face and told me I had to tell the Foreman, George Gooding, what had happened when he came on at 8 am. George came in, sucking his pipe and wandered around to see the wreckage of 941 and our Land Rover. I was expecting the sack at least. George just laughed and said "hopefully you'll learn from this"! I never hooked up a bus again without checking the handbrake worked.

From the public's perspective North Western had a special place in the communities served. Peter Whitworth's upbringing in Matlock was to a background of NWRCC buses:

One regular "appointment" in my teens was to visit the railway bridge over Dale Road just after 8pm on Sundays. Buses were more popular then, because the number 4 service between Derby and Buxton passing north often had up to four duplicates, at least some taking day trippers home from Matlock Bath. Occasionally one might be Trent, presumably because North Western were short of vehicles. We regarded Trent as "foreigners" and were very disappointed if they came along! While we were there we'd see a southbound express train pass at speed, being the only train all week to not stop at Matlock station, of which my Grandfather had once been stationmaster.

I'll always remember two things. The first was the depot on Bakewell Road in Matlock – the left side was used operationally, the right side was used for storage. Imagine my shock one day when I peered into the slightly open door of the right side of the garage, to find ten or a dozen brand new Leyland Tiger Cubs in the KDB series. At least some worked in the area for a while, but I was told later that they were replaced by older Royal Tigers because the local hills were too much for the smaller Cub engines.

My second recollection was again on the number 4 service. Sometimes the service would only go as far as Rowsley (pronounced "Rose-Lee") with ROWSLEY on the front. But I couldn't believe it when a North Western car came into Matlock with the blind set for RAWSLEY – perhaps someone on the end of a phone line taking instructions misheard the village's name?

On the platform, the job was a fund of stories. In 1966, Stuart Barker was a student working as a conductor for the summer. He recalls one day in 1966 above all others:

> This was one of the most enjoyable periods of my life. The drivers I worked with were a great group of people – as were the passengers, on the whole.
>
> One date stands out – 30 July 1966, World Cup Final day. I was working "lates" and watched the first 90 minutes of the game at home then walked to the Market Place bus station before the extra time period. Buses were parked up but there wasn't a soul to be seen – neither crews nor public. There was nobody in the office; nobody in the canteen. So, I went upstairs to the Social Club (where I'd never ventured before). And there they were! You couldn't move for the crowd of staff watching the television. I was on the half-hourly 27 service to Manchester but departure time came and went, and no driver appeared. I called from the back of the crowd "is anybody on Manchesters?" and a muffled reply "yes, I am" was heard. "Are we leaving?" "No, we're not." And that was that! We left about five minutes before the following departure, but none of the very few passengers complained. They knew that in general we did our best for them, so they did their best for us.

Yes, North Western was a friendly company.

Let's start at number 1 – unusually, it was second-hand. This Bristol K5G was supplied to neighbour Potteries, who got it during the war when buses were allocated by the Ministry of War Transport. NWRCC got a couple of equally unwelcome Daimlers, so a swap was arranged.

North Western had no female platform staff before 1940, and in fact never employed a lady bus driver, but with men joining the Forces, wartime clippies were employed. This is a rare photo taken during the war years, possibly at Winsford.

It's 1949 and Manchester's Kingsway is having its Corporation tram standards and tracks removed – the city's last tram had recently clanked this way. A North Western Bristol speeds by, hurrying past on the 30 service from Macclesfield.

This was what North Western was about – a Bristol in red and cream; shame about the black and white photo! All was not what it seemed: the body and the radiator was new, but underneath lurked a 1938 chassis, modernised and rebodied to get the last pennies of value from the indestructible Bristol.

This is our first visit to Manchester Lower Mosley Street. These Bristol K5Gs were the heart of the company's double deck services for many years. Power from the five-cylinder Gardner engine wasn't outstanding, but timings for the 28 to Hayfield were generous.

Although the Willowbrook rebodied Bristols were famous, there was also a fair number of Guy 'Arab' buses bought during the war and also given a rebuild. 22 looks smart in this photo, so hopefully didn't need the services of the tow lorry on the left...

...which was, yet again, an old Bristol that was taken into Charles Street and given this homemade body. It was known to all as the 'Brab', probably after the impressive Brabazon airliner that was also a machine of great bulk.

North Western posed a before-and-after photo to show how the rebuilds were a better prospect than the originals. No doubt a particularly disreputable specimen was chosen for the 'before', but the contrast was clear.

Out of time sequence, just to pay a courtesy call, is the parking ground at Stockport's Daw Bank. Hemmed in by Wellington Road South, the River Mersey, the viaduct and a hat factory, it was also on a slope. More than one bus set off on an unbidden journey.

Away from Manchester, North Western served many rural outposts and suffered from extreme weather. This is Monsal Top in 1947, the worst winter in living memory, and it was several days before this Bristol L5G made it to Buxton.

In the 1950s the firm's favoured coachbuilder was Weymann. Head office worker Philip Edwards captured delivery day from his office window. Left to right are a Leyland PD2; an AEC Reliance with 'Fanfare' coach body; and a Tiger Cub bus.

Not all services in Cheshire were rural: one of the biggest garages was at Northwich where salt extraction and chemical works kept North Western busy. One of the Bristol K5Gs awaited the early shift in 1962, while a Tiger Cub lurked at the end of the street.

North Western's premier express service was the X5 group to London, most of which involved a refreshment stop at the 'Four in Hand' café at Newcastle-under-Lyme. It was owned by fellow BET company Potteries, so profits from all those cups of tea were kept in the family.

The Bristols soldiered on well into the 1960s, by which time they looked like antiques (which they were). They still looked a brave sight after repainting like number 435 at Charles Street, even if the red roof didn't look as good as the cream original.

The first new double-deckers delivered after the war were Leyland PD1 buses with Eastern Coach Works bodies. The PD1's slow gear change was hard work in hilly areas while the bodies used poor quality wood. They went long before the older Bristols.

In Stockport's Mersey Square, NWRCC jostled with Stockport buses plus visitors from Manchester, Ashton and Stalybridge. The 27 was 'by arrangement' with Manchester to protect the city's buses but this wouldn't worry the crew on a short working from Stockport to New Mills.

Let's just take one more look at those glorious Willowbrook rebodies – this time in an official view of number 20 taken by the coachbuilder. Doesn't 20 look a fine sight?

This is 20 again, at the other end of its career. Earlier in life this would have been repaired but by the time this happened, it was the end. The damage has given us a look at the Gardner 5LW diesel engine – not over-powered but beloved of fleet engineers for its reliability and economy.

After the war North Western bought many Bristol L5G buses almost identical to the pre-war version. The early post-war bodies weren't over-robust, being made with unseasoned timber, and number 90 here was given this Weymann body in the 1950s.

Unlike Ribble, NWRCC didn't create a bureaucracy and this modest headquarters sufficed until the end. Located on Charles Street across from the works and garage, it later became the office for Greater Manchester's Charterplan unit.

If the 1940s were defined by Bristol K5G and L5G buses, the 1950s were defined by underfloor-engined models, mainly with bodies by Weymann, like 537. It was a Leyland Royal Tiger, and buses like it were seen in every corner of the company's territory for years.

Matlock garage was a neat affair made up of two main bays. In this view the Enquiries Office had put posters in the window advertising Skegness, Llandudno and Rhyl, but holidaymakers were starting to explore Benidorm and Torremolinos.

When underfloor-engined buses arrived, what NWRCC wanted was a Bristol but they'd been nationalised. Atkinson of Preston could provide something similar, featuring a Gardner engine. After a few had been bought, BET made it clear that orders must switch to AEC and Leyland.

659 was a Tiger Cub at Hulme Hall Road garage in Manchester and judging by the blind it had been used for a 'dupe' on a long-distance run. The coach behind was definitely on a long-distance job from Northern – the fellow BET company based in Gateshead – and was probably refuelling.

It's 1955, we're in Fairfield Road in Buxton and a North Western car is heading under the Midland Railway branch from the town to Millers Dale. There was a passenger service until 1967 and it is still open today to serve the quarries at Dowlow.

North Western's Oldham services were a bit of an outpost; in the beginning there was no connection to the rest of the company's network. The garage was busy enough to support some double-deckers including 407, which looks in need of a repaint.

Although the K5Gs looked great on the outside, the interior was different. This view upstairs on preserved 432 shows the narrow sunken gangway, the low ceiling and the benches of four seats to achieve an overall height of 13 feet 4 inches.

For most of its history, North Western buses were a cut above Corporation buses in its area. They were comfier and had deeper seats, even in the austerity days after the war. 132 was a case in point and was new in 1946. Although it looked great, the bodywork quality was shaky, and all were either rebodied or scrapped in the 1950s.

The Leyland Royal Tiger coaches of 1952 were regarded as the 'top' fleet when they arrived. Their livery was more attractive than the huge army of the same type delivered to Ribble at the same time, and they spent most of their early years on London trips. 607 has escaped however, to Llandudno.

Mersey Square, at peak hour. It's the swinging sixties, but even at that date every evening would bring queues like this to the company's services. It was easy to see how profitable and busy services like the 81 were used to subsidise the rural network.

The 'HJA' AEC Reliances were slightly odd men out; instead of sturdy Weymann bodies they had less robust ones by Burlingham. Drivers hated them for being cold, and few tears were shed when they finally departed.

This bus was delivered to Rochdale Corporation in 1938 and on withdrawal was sold to Cowley, the Salford dealer that North Western also used, and was bought by NWRCC for conversion to a mobile canteen.

Here it is on completion, fitted out to a high standard by Charles Street. For years it drove each morning from Hulme Hall Road garage to Lower Mosley Street bus station and was used as a staff canteen, driving back again each evening.

One of the first Atkinson buses got an outing on the MIRA test track near Nuneaton. They were solid buses, although not with the best brakes, and the gearbox linkage tended to get loose over time. North Western liked them, the BET Head Office did not.

Although the Atkinsons were underfloor-engined, the door was at the rear. Virtually all the company's buses had rear entrances, so at the time this seemed logical. Not surprisingly, the front nearside has already been bagged for the trip to Buxton.

Leyland's competitor was the 'Olympic' made with partners Metro Cammell Weymann. A rear door wasn't available but, in any case, the front door proved to be superior. Thereafter all single-deckers bought by NWRCC came with front doors.

The new Charles Street fuelling area shows the 1950s company in a state of flux – most buses on show are Bristol L5Gs, but in the depot you can just see a couple of underfloor-engined ones. The pale building in the background is Brookfield House, which was a children's home.

The last front-engined Bristols to be delivered arrived in 1950, quite a while after Bristol was nationalised but the firm could complete orders that had already been placed. Even when they were new, they weren't the last word in modernity.

When NWRCC needed a van to transport uniforms it used an old Bristol bus and gave it a homemade body. And of course, it carried a 'travel by coach' slogan! E986 was seen outside the Head Office at Charles Street.

The door closed to buying Bristol and Eastern Coach Works when they were nationalised. The post-war combination was common in former Tilling fleets, but only one batch for North Western carried this attractive style.

You wouldn't call Northwich bus station 'pretty', and the garage works on the right can't have improved the environment, but at least everyone got home on one of the buses in the background, including three Guys and four Bristols.

Bristol supplied coaches too; the coachwork was by Windover of Huntingdon. Within a few years they were made to look old-fashioned by new underfloor-engined models. The wood frames started to rot, so they were gone by the end of the 1950s.

The first big batch of double-deckers to arrive after the war was a set of Leyland PD2s with Leyland bodies. There were few opening windows, which led to complaints, so after a time they received one front ventilator giving them a lopsided appearance.

Above and below: The following 'deckers' were more PD2s but this time with Weymann bodies. They were proper lookers when new, but over time they were rebuilt with rubber-mounted windows, which turned them from the prettiest buses in the fleet to the ugliest.

One of the 1953 Leylands was sent to Lincoln to receive an air-cooled engine by Ruston &
Hornsby and is seen here in that city. Its appearance and sound weren't forgotten in a hurry and
it was converted back.

Even the CDB Leylands weren't immune from Charles Street's liking for rubber window
mounts; 231 acquired some rebuilt windows towards the end. You can make your own
mind up if it improved the appearance, but then North Western was always good at
make-do-and-mend.

As the 1950s progressed, staff turnover rose as wages fell behind other industries. So a fleet of time-expired buses was kept to train new drivers such as 942 here, which came out of passenger service but lingered on as a trainer until 1958.

Redundant Bristol chassis were far too good to throw away – they wore out much more slowly than their bodies. So 984 became a lorry for transporting spares and bus stops, with a little platform for tree lopping. It was sold for scrap in 1968.

The Burlingham 'Seagull' body was a classic. They were ideal for services such as the X2 to Nottingham, which ran jointly with Trent and (on some journeys) was linked to an X60 to Blackpool, creating a through Nottingham–Blackpool service.

304 hadn't been to London for a long time; in fact it had probably never been. But despite being in the autumn of its days it still looked quite smart even though, by then, the economics of a thirty-five-seat bus with a two-man crew were hopeless.

Afternoon at Lower Mosley Street bus station, Manchester. A 27 to Buxton and a 32 to Middlewood await departure. Both services ran every half hour through the day. The Buxton would leave on the hour and the half past, while the Middlewood would depart five minutes later.

If the Weymann 'Fanfare' wasn't the prettiest coach body of the 1950s, it was probably in the top three. 570 was the first to be built and was on display at the 1954 Commercial Motor Show before entering service.

The rear view of the 'Fanfare' body didn't work quite as well, but they were liked by passengers and built very solidly. 570 even got a high-speed rear axle differential in 1961 for the new motorways, before bowing out in 1964.

During the 1950s, NWRCC embarked on a set of body swaps in its single deck Bristols so that the best bodies were on the best chassis, and the least good were sold. This is a 1946 bus that (in 1957) was given a 1952 Willowbrook body, which had originally been mounted on a 1938 chassis!

Even Bristol L5G buses have to die, and during the 1950s the usual replacement was this: a Leyland Tiger Cub with Weymann body. This one is in Macclesfield bus station after a fourteen-minute journey from Langley.

Earlier we saw a Weymann Fanfare coach; here's its rival, a Burlingham 'Seagull' type mounted on a Tiger Cub chassis. The Seagull was distinctly heavyweight, and the Tiger Cub was definitely lightweight, with only 5.74 litres of diesel power under the floor.

We saw a Royal Tiger coach with Leyland body earlier. They were uncertain in the braking department, and it's not a coincidence that over the years they all got front end rebuilds. The front seat wouldn't stay vacant for long on the trip to Derby.

Later in the 1950s, British coach body design lost its way a little and although the products of Harrington of Hove were of top quality, it's fair to say that the 'Wayfarer' design wasn't the company's finest hour. But NWRCC cream and red suited almost anything.

We've seen rural scenes but here's one at the other end of the spectrum. The 79 ran every twenty minutes between Stockport and Cheadle Hulme and Mersey Square just by the Plaza cinema, which was showing *Hot Enough for June*, starring Dirk Bogarde.

After sale 710 found a new life in South Wales with Hills of Tredegar. It went there in 1967 when ten years old, which was the usual age North Western let coaches go, and Hill kept the red and cream as it was similar to his own livery.

This is Oldham, which was North Western territory but seemed slightly out-of-the-way. But several profitable services were based from its garage here in Crofton Street, just south of the town centre.

514 has come to grief at Topley Pike on the A6 between Buxton and Bakewell, and it'll take more than the 'Brab' to get it out of its predicament. 514 went on to be repaired and, without irony, became a driver trainer at the end of its service.

678 was a Tiger Cub with mesh-covered holes in the front panel. This wasn't a big problem on this type generally, but on long hill climbs the little engine could start getting slightly hot and bothered.

743 has arrived at Lower Mosley Street after a run on the X67 from Chesterfield. Looking at the shadows it's likely to be the 11 o'clock departure, arriving in Manchester at 1.08 pm. It seems to be a lovely day for a trip across the Peak District.

Windover built coach bodies for the Bristol L5G but also on Leyland PS2 chassis – the only ones of this type to be bought by NWRCC. They were more powerful than the Bristols, but they lacked the Bristol overdrive fifth gear and the bodies rotted prematurely.

Cowley's of Salford took hundreds of old NWRCC buses and coaches over the years. 740 to 745 were sold on to Wimpeys who used them to transport workers to new home estates or roads. 743 was scrapped, worn out, in 1971.

An official photo of the new bus wash at Charles Street gives us the chance to study the rear of 687, fitted with flashing trafficators and a small boot below the emergency exit, which was ideal for market day crates and baskets.

For some years NWRCC operated two coaching subsidiaries in blue and cream: Altrincham Coachways and Melba Motors of Reddish. Coaches were allocated from a batch bought by the parent company and 703 did a few months as a red coach before being transferred to Melba.

A typical view for a passenger for most of the 1950s and 1960s – the seats are upholstered in moquette in shades of red with leather trimming, and like almost all the company's single-deckers it has luggage racks for rural and longer services.

In the late 1950s, inspired by Midland Red, NWRCC tried a new livery for 'dual purpose' vehicles i.e. those with a standard bus body but with more comfortable seats for express and longer services. Known as 'black tops', they looked the business.

In 1958, North Western found itself short of coaches; it asked Willowbrook, then building ten 'black top' vehicles, to paint them in full coach livery. To be fair they also got slightly more comfy seats but after a few years they were repainted.

The black tops were meant for longer services, but they could be found on almost any route. 762 is a case in point as it's working the Uppermill Circular. The (M.P.) on the blind stood for Market Place.

When the first batch of black tops were downgraded for bus use in the 1960s the effect was depressing. 736 still retained its nice seats for the run from Manchester to Buxton; it now looked like just any old bus, which in truth, it was.

Most black tops later got this paint scheme which was the dual-purpose livery for the last years of North Western's existence. It didn't look bad, although an older DP bus wasn't an ideal choice for the X97 Liverpool–Newcastle service.

Later still, some back tops got a standard red paint job with cream relief. The side mouldings were painted over and 764 looks quite dusty and uncared for in this shot taken in Trumpet Street a few yards from Lower Mosley Street bus station.

The last surviving PD2 with Leyland body became a trainer at Charles Street. It lasted for years, and by the time NWRCC was split up it was by far the oldest bus in the fleet even if it wasn't used for passenger service. We'll see it again later.

The last Leyland double-deckers had lowbridge Weymann 'Orion' bodies. They were unpopular because they were cramped, had a hard ride and the small windows meant that passengers couldn't see out. No wonder this one was registered 666!

The most south-eastern outpost of NWRCC territory was Derby, terminus of the 4 from Buxton run jointly with Trent. 633 was a Buxton car for many years and was photographed at Derby's Art Deco bus station which was sadly demolished in 2006.

The last Bristol L5G buses were based at Altrincham because a canal aqueduct bridge at Dunham Massey was too low for underfloor-engined buses. This was good news for 270, as it lasted through a series of contractors to be preserved and restored.

829 was in Blackpool in August 1969. As buses in rural areas declined, express services and coach hire became more popular. 829 was based at Stockport but often, on a holiday weekend, coaches and buses were borrowed from other garages to fulfil a private hire.

Pride in the job! With Fred Fildes as conductor and Fred Read as driver, the crew get ready for the one hour forty minute run to Buxton. Fred Read was renowned for offering to do 'double shifts', or in other words do a morning shift till early afternoon then do another one into the evening!

North Western buses had a good reputation on the second-hand market, and many ended up as contractor buses or used by scout groups and schools. The latter destination awaited 791.

The location is Southport which is the terminus of the 309 service. But the other end isn't Stockport but St Helens, and the 309 was joint between St Helens Corporation and Ribble! Did North Western lend a coach to help out its neighbour for the day?

North Western couldn't have the Bristol 'Lodekka' as Bristol was nationalised. But when Dennis of Guildford launched a licensed version as the 'Loline', NW bought some and loaned one of the first ones to Aldershot & District, which had Lolines but wanted to try the front entrance version.

The Lolines allowed 'normal' seating upstairs instead of the lowbridge layout. 816 was on one of its first runs at Lower Mosley Street and it's unclear whether the gent by the door is impressed or wondering how he's going to get around to collect the fares.

813 came to grief fairly early in life near to the Shell-Mex complex at Carrington. A fitter has come out from Urmston in the depot's Land Rover, but it'll take a lot more than that to extract 813 from its position.

In 1961 a batch of AEC Reliances with Alexander bodies was delivered, dubbed 'Highlanders'. They were to be seen everywhere including the X5 to London, although they were prone to head gasket failure when used on long non-stop runs.

From the rear the Highlanders looked slightly old-fashioned, but they were a neat job. North Western didn't over advertise themselves on their coaches; this batch carried no name on the rear at all unlike the coach in front – it was all very classy.

North Western's policy was to downgrade coaches after a few years and by 1969, 832 was in the half-and-half livery at Lower Mosley Street, on a trip to Higher Poynton where once it would have departed to London Victoria.

The second batch of Dennis Lolines carried bodies by Alexander, who were becoming a favoured supplier for BET in general, and North Western in particular. Each one as it arrived replaced a Bristol K5G but the passengers knew which they preferred.

Macclesfield, with Lolines hoovering up shoppers. At least one would be on the 29/30 services to Manchester which would give an exhilarating countryside run from Macclesfield west to Monks Heath, then up the A34 to Alderley Edge and Wilmslow.

The Lolines were worked very hard, so let's skip forward to July 1976. 887 was by then owned by SELNEC and dumped at Manchester's Bennett Street yard. After withdrawal the Gardner engine probably lived on in a boat or as a fairground generator.

In the late 1950s, the company put some investment into its garages. A new one was opened at Biddulph joint with PMT. Wilmslow was relocated and, as we see here, Buxton was moved into a new site close to the station. It closed under Trent ownership and a supermarket now stands on its site.

For its next double-deckers, North Western turned to AEC. The choice was the 'Renown', a competitor in the lowheight market, and the contract for bodywork went to Park Royal of London. The result was solid and purposeful.

Two rivals for North Western's affections – Dennis on the left, AEC on the right. They enabled a normal upstairs seating layout unlike the Bristols they replaced. And with nearly twenty more seats, two buses like this could replace three Bristol K5Gs.

The next batch of coaches were Leyland Leopards, which became the choice for coach purchases until the end. The body was the same Alexander style as the AEC Reliances but to the new maximum 36-foot length. The location is Daw Bank.

Just as with most other coaches, after a few years they were given the dual-purpose livery. It looks like 909 is in between duties on the five-times-a-day service to Bramhall (North Park), so a nice ride for its shopper passengers.

The last of the Bristol L5Gs needed replacing so AEC provided these Reliances with Willowbrook bodywork. They were the first to arrive with curved windscreens to a design called the 'BET screen' because it was developed for North Western's owners.

Stockport Mersey Square at rush hour and one of the new AECs shares the stand with a Highlander on the last stop from London before arriving in Manchester. There is also a Loline, and two Stockport Corporation buses.

There was a second half to the batch of Willowbrooks; they had two fewer seats and were known to crews as 'flying bananas' due to their striking livery, which sadly wasn't expanded to other vehicles.

We're skipping forward in time to see one near the end of its life, working for Greater Manchester Transport but carrying SELNEC fleetnames and NWRCC livery. It's a great shame that none survives.

By 1963, Alexander was in a position to replace the Highlander with something special – the Y-type. Equally at home on short excursions or the London express, it became the standard express vehicle for the rest of the company's existence.

For really prestigious jobs, NWRCC would turn out 962 or 963 – Leyland Leopards with Plaxton bodies, complete with chrome-raised fleetnames on the side. 962 was entering Oxford's Gloucester Green bus station on the X5E to London.

Bedfords didn't really feature in the North Western fleet but a few were bought for Altrincham Coachways including this one, which was only transferred to the parent company and given the number 996 for its last few months before being sold in 1967.

Above and below: North Western didn't like the semi-lowbridge layout offered by the Leyland Atlantean, so when the Daimler Fleetline came along with a low height and normal seating, it became the company's standard. Alexander did a handsome job on the bodywork.

The Fleetlines soon settled down to service on the company's busiest routes such as the 23 to Flixton (Red Lion). 113 displays a short-lived 1960s fad – an illuminated advert panel on the offside, which was meant to attract a higher advertising rate.

North Western hedged its bets when ordering the Fleetlines – it wasn't clear at the time that it would be a complete success. So a second batch of AEC Renowns arrived; they were good buses but just seemed old-fashioned in comparison.

The last Bristols departed from Altrincham garage in 1964. Their replacements were specially built Bedford VAL buses with arched-roof Strachans bodies, which meant a lower overall height that would fit under the canal bridge at Dunham Massey.

Here's Dunham Massey bridge. Headroom was tighter at the far end, leading to the 8-foot 9-inch restriction, which the VALs could dip under but higher underfloor-engined buses couldn't.

All the Bedfords were sent to Altrincham, which was more than was needed for the service that went under the bridge, so they also ended up on other trips as required such as the Hale Barns circular.

By the 1960s, NWRCC was looking thoroughly modern. This official view shows Urmston garage with a new Fleetline in the doorway. But the truth was that NWRCC was already in decline, having been squeezed by rising labour costs and increasing car ownership.

A third batch of Fleetlines arrived in 1965. 188 was slightly different in that it arrived with an experimental heating system that created the blank panel just ahead of the rear axle, but it wasn't adopted as standard.

Chester Zoo, 1967, and one of the drivers of the excursion from Stockport seems to be checking his instructions. Private hire was a profitable activity and it probably helped stave off closure of some rural services.

When the 'Brab' wore out, an ex-military AEC Matador was bought at auction. It was stripped down to the chassis and overhauled; the old crane was mounted; and new bodywork made using many Alexander parts.

Every year, the company's directors would do a tour of the company's garages. This is the 1964 tour at Charles Street, as they inspect a new Y-type Leopard. The man in overalls on the right was probably keeping his own counsel.

The X5L was the Manchester–London via Altrincham, Newcastle-under-Lyme, Birmingham and towns along the A5 service. Through passengers – not many on an eight-and-a-half-hour journey – got refreshment stops at Newcastle and Digbeth.

The premier London service was the X5Z, using as much of the motorway network as it could and taking just five and a half hours. This photo captures the 17.15 departure, while the X97 next to it is probably a duplicate for the 17.35 departure.

By contrast the X5M was the overnight coach, with stops at Newcastle, Birmingham and St Albans. The service left London at 23.30, arriving with its load of weary travellers in Lower Mosley Street at 07.45 the next morning.

The next batch of excursion coaches were Leopards with beautiful Harrington 'Grenadier' bodies. They could be seen on express services, but their real trade was extended holidays, tours and excursions.

The company's standards slipped during the late 1950s but investment in garages and new buses helped turn the situation around. This is the new workshop at Hulme Hall Road, Manchester, with new Fleetline 179 sampling the sunken maintenance area.

At last, the restriction on buying Bristol buses was lifted and NWRCC was at the front of the queue, ordering 40 RESL6G models for delivery in 1968. This is 276, one of the first, setting off on a trip over the Pennines.

Sadly, 276 didn't get far! In May 1969, when less than a year old, 276 caught fire on the Saddleworth moors and burned to a crisp. It never ran again.

The 28 to Hayfield competed with a British Railways branch line, which had been opened in 1868. Judging by 167's load there wasn't even enough traffic for the bus, so it was no surprise when the railway closed in 1970.

Beautiful, flowing curves … serenity personified … and there are also some swans. 235 was driven to Lyme Park at Disley for some official photos and very nice it looked, too.

Duple hadn't featured in North Western's orders but its 'Commander' body started to appear on the usual Leyland Leopard chassis. They were popular with drivers, being regarded as 'flying machines' for long trips like this one to Oxford.

The AECs formed the bulk of the double deck fleet at Northwich – three can be seen peeping out of the garage doors. 976, on the right, has had a spell on the 234 service, the Northwich circular town service.

Fleetlines continued to arrive through the mid-1960s. On busy summer days they were useful crowd-shifters on the busy X60 Blackpool service, and it's likely that 196 has just dropped a load of returning trippers from the resort.

Eastbourne is a long way from Manchester, but brand new 257 would manage it, and would probably spend most of the M1 section north from London in the outside lane at 80 mph, as this was long before the days of speed limiters.

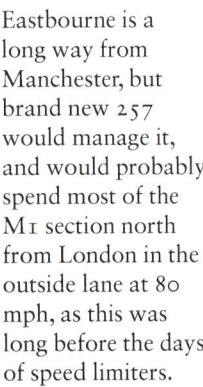

NWRCC ordered ten Y-types every year, and they would spend the first couple of years on the X5 services to London before being relegated to easier work. The X5E variant was a ten-hour grueller via Birmingham and Oxford.

You can almost hear the tinkle of knives and forks and the chatter of the crews from the canteen at Glossop depot in 1966. The depot was on the edge of the town, surrounded by fields on three sides, but busy enough to justify quite a few double deckers.

Marshall of Cambridge was proud of getting orders from North Western and created publicity postcards showing 295A. The 'A' meant 'bus equipped for one-man operation' but by the turn of the decade most buses were, so the suffix was dropped.

'Hurry up Jim, he's goin'!' Probably not as 221 looks fairly empty and is probably quite a while off departure. The rear of the Alexander Y-type was as well-designed as the front; modern, purposeful, practical.

When longer REs were required for 1969 and 1970, it was natural to choose the bus version of the Y-type but still with the sloping panoramic windows. They were very handsome, but you had to be rather tall to see out of the seats near the front.

The last Fleetlines arrived in 1967 and in 1970, four of them were painted in this 'reversed' livery for use on the X60 alongside Ribble's 'White Lady' Atlanteans. But inside they were standard, with no luggage compartment or high-backed seats.

The Dunham Massey Bedford VALs wore out after a few years (they were only lightweight) and in 1971 a batch of Bristol REs was bought to replace them with low roof design. Here they are at Charles Street before being sent over to Altrincham.

Here's the obligatory 'under Dunham Massey bridge' photo. Shortly afterwards the bridge started to collapse and was rebuilt with more headroom, removing the need for special buses.

From the rear the low REs looked even more odd than the front. The appearance was pleasing overall, but the structure was a bodge job by ECW and they were withdrawn and scrapped at a fairly young age.

The last hurrah for the garage rebuild programme was the new combined garage and bus station on Clegg Street in Oldham, opened in 1966. Sadly, it was closed after the split-up so lasted less than ten years.

Ten Y-types a year continued to arrive until the end of the company's existence. The last set delivered in 1971 had a revised front end that your author happens to think made them the most handsome of all.

For 1971's Bristol REs a return was made to Marshall for the bodywork. Here's the batch all lined up at Charles Street, but they weren't licensed before the August registration changeover date so all the reg. plates had to be replaced by K-suffix ones.

Here's 357 in service at Northwich. Photos of them in full NWRCC are rare as they all passed within a few months to Crosville and Trent who painted them quickly.

Above and below: For touring in 1971, NWRCC turned to Plaxton and took official photos at Charles Street complete with Head Office staff pretending to be passengers. Some of these Leopards were delivered with forty-five seats but within a few months an extra row had been squeezed in.

The last buses (as opposed to coaches) to be delivered in NWRCC livery were Bristol REs with ECW bodies, but standard height this time, which were in course of delivery when the split-up came. They went to Crosville who painted them in green very quickly.

The changeover in two pictures. The first photo shows 405 at Lower Mosley Street, in cream and red with the proud fleetname on its side. The second shows 403 at Hulme Hall Road just a few months later, in insipid white with a tiny 'North Western' over the wheel arch.

What a garage engineer likes to see: an almost empty depot, in this case at Oldham. But it isn't Clegg Street, it's the former Corporation depot, and 'Flying Banana' 939 shares the shed with SELNEC buses.

Crosville made a strong effort to repaint its North Western acquisitions quickly, and by September 1972 former NWRCC 896 was in Tilling green at Macclesfield bus station as DEG401 (the DEG meant double-decker, Loline, Gardner engine).

SELNEC seemed a lot less bothered about repainting and on 15 April 1972, at Altrincham, it was hard to tell that there'd been a change. The North Western fleetname on the side was gone, but there was no clue as to the new owner of 868.

Eventually SELNEC started to repaint its fleet with 'CHESHIRE' flashes on the sides, which was not wholly appropriate for 301, at Glossop, as that splendid town was, and is, firmly in Derbyshire.

Above and below: At the time of dissolution, the company had twenty-five Bristol VR buses on order, and they would have been the first buses in NBC Poppy Red. Instead the order was taken on by SELNEC and they were painted orange and off-white.

Winter was coming literally and metaphorically at Urmston (177 is on the Eccles), the Levenshulme service now diverted away from the low Barton aqueduct that had claimed at least one NWRCC double-decker roof.

There was still pride in the job, of course, but the 'CHESHIRE' flash just wasn't the same as the old North Western fleetname, and when applied to red buses like 787 the brown fleetname just blended in.

The last batch of Fleetlines went to Crosville except the cream painted ones which (bizarrely) stayed with the residual coaching NWRCC until they were quickly transferred to City of Oxford. 250 was repainted in full Tilling green.

Once upon a time 912 thundered along the M6 and M1 on the X5Z, the premier London service. In January 1973 it was working nine-minute trips to Sinderland Estate. How are the mighty fallen!

The very last vehicles to be delivered in NWRCC cream and red were five REs with ECW coach bodies, which were delivered after the rump of North Western became a coach-only firm. They were workmanlike but somehow lacked the panache of the Y-type.

This 1973 scene at Urmston shows an almost totally orange fleet with a couple of ex-Manchester buses transferred in. The one lurking to the right of 176 is a Leyland Atlantean, a type that NWRCC never bought.

The next step was the renumbering of former North Western services. For many years Hayfield had been the terminus of the 28 from Manchester, but under SELNEC it was cut back to Stockport and renumbered 358.

The low height REs went to Crosville at their Warrington depot and mainly stayed there, even though the low bridge that they were built for was now rebuilt. 379 – now SRL244 – rested at Urmston on the Warrington service.

The last vehicles to be delivered with 'North Western' on the side was a batch of five 1973 Leopards with Duple 'Dominant' bodies in white. In February 1974 the company was renamed to the catchy 'National Travel (North West) Ltd' and that was that.

Even though there were still red buses, especially in the SELNEC area, the winds of change blew hard. Urmston garage was an early casualty in 1973 and its allocation and staff moved to Manchester's Princess Road depot.

The VRs worked from the former Stockport Corporation depot at Daw Bank but, even though they were delivered with the standard SELNEC destination gear, crews refused to use the 'via' blind, so they were painted over for quite a while.

The very last red and cream bus in service was Fleetline 1, given the same number by SELNEC and seen here working from Oldham. It wasn't painted orange until 1976, over four years after NWRCC had been split up.

As the red and cream livery went, so did the vehicles. Although the Bristol RE on the left doesn't have a front panel, in fact, it's 944 that's withdrawn at the back of Altrincham garage in July 1975.

Now it was a coach-only company, North Western couldn't cascade older coaches on to bus work. So a small group of 1968 Y-types went to Ribble, where they could be seen on the former NWRCC X12 service.

SELNEC gave way to Greater Manchester Transport in 1974. GMT liked to move its buses around and although former 110 and 101 were found at the ex-NW Altrincham garage, they ended their days at Frederick Road and Northenden respectively.

The Y-types that went to Crosville were given this fairly attractive NBC dual purpose livery, and Macclesfield's ELL323 (ex-MWRCC 215) was found in Manchester Piccadilly on the E30 service – formerly the 30 – back to its hometown.

Trent took over operations from Buxton and Matlock garages plus the little outstation at Castleton, and very little looked different at first. Former NWRCC 930 was now Trent 373 but Buxton Market Place looked the same.

Greater Manchester Transport built a small bus station in Hayfield on the site of the railway station that the buses had helped kill off. 280 visited the still unfinished facility on what was the truncated remains of the Glossop–Buxton service.

Trent's pre-NBC dual-purpose livery was quite effective, arguably more so than North Western's half-and-half scheme. Former NWRCC 216 wore the scheme well at Buxton garage on 16 April 1972.

Crosville's allocation changed colour again from Tilling green to NBC Leaf Green, and former 304 looks creditable in Macclesfield bus station. Most of this batch went to SELNEC but the final few went to Crosville.

By 1976 the last few remnants were disappearing. Lower Mosley St closed in 1973, its tattiness replaced by the concrete gloom of Chorlton Street coach station. 259 was one of the last coaches to retain the 'North Western' name.

All of the Y-type Bristol REs went to SELNEC, so rural views weren't usual. But some of the area around Partington and Carrington is quite green and 319 actually looked quite smart when seen in July 1975.

Trent was a 'red' company, so when NBC made all of its subsidiaries choose from Leaf Green or Poppy Red, Trent chose the latter as we see on former 217 in Stockport. One assumes that had it survived North Western would have gone the same way.

Crosville chose Leaf Green and its DDG308 (NWRCC 195) looks quite smart. But not all is well: a seat cushion leaning on the rear was a traditional way of signalling to following traffic that the bus was broken down and not going anywhere soon.

Many employees served for very many years. Second from left is driver Bob Binns, who spent almost his whole career with NWRCC at Matlock. He acted as a TGWU rep and could be found most Decembers acting as Father Christmas for the garage's annual Christmas party.

1958? No, 2018 at the Museum of Transport Greater Manchester. This is Leyland PD2 224 and behind it, Bristol 432. It's good that they and other preserved NWRCC buses keep the company's name alive.

In 2019 this bus stop remained in situ and in use somewhere in the former company's area, although best not to say where. It's good to know that somewhere out there the North Western is still helping travellers.

NORTH WESTERN